W0081672

REENA ESMAIL
Sŭnāō

Three songs on the power of listening and connection
with original Hindi texts by Reena Bhansali

for SAB and piano

vocal score

CONTENTS

OXFORD
UNIVERSITY PRESS

Sŭnāō was commissioned by the following consortium of choirs through the Southern California Vocal Association:

Ramón C. Cortines School of Visual and Performing Arts—Drew Lewis, Choral Director
South Bay Children's Choir—Julie Corallo, Artistic Director
VOX Femina Los Angeles—Dr Iris S. Levine, Founding Artistic Director
Arroyo High School—Jennifer Stanley, Choral Director
Young Naperville Singers—Angie Johnson, Artistic Director
Irvine High School—Tina Glander Peterson, Choral Director
Palisades Charter High School—Allison Cheng, Choral Director
Magnolia High School—Alan Garcia, Choral Director
Norco High School—Antone Rodich, Choral Director
Ramona Middle School—Caitlin Shaw, Choral Director
Ramona High School—Jennifer Phillips, Choral Director
Herbert Hoover High School—Amy Estep, Choral Director
Mira Costa High School—Kate Crellin, Choral Director
Oak Park High School—Stacy McClamma, Choral Director
San Dimas High School Choir Department—Jared Pugh, Choral Director
San Fernando Valley Youth Chorus—Marisa Bradfield, Artistic Director
Providence High School—Marisa Bradfield, Choral Director
Girls Academic Leadership Academy—Heather Leppard, Choral Director
Piedmont East Bay Children's Choir—Eric Tuan, Artistic Director
Oregon Repertory Singers—Lauren Bryan, Artistic Director
Gilroy High School and Christopher High School—Jonathan Souza, Choral Director
Sauk Rapids-Rice High School Choirs—Steven D. Mick, Choral Director
Blue Mountain Middle School—Kimberly Dunkin, Choral Director
Concordia University, Irvine—Dr Clarissa Shan, Choral Director

OXFORD
UNIVERSITY PRESS

Great Clarendon Street, Oxford OX2 6DP,
United Kingdom

Oxford University Press is a department of the University of Oxford.
It furthers the University's objective of excellence in research, scholarship,
and education by publishing worldwide. Oxford is a registered trade mark of
Oxford University Press in the UK and in certain other countries

© Oxford University Press 2025

Reena Esmail has asserted her right under the Copyright, Designs
and Patents Act, 1988, to be identified as the Composer of this Work

First published 2025

All rights reserved. No part of this publication may be reproduced,
stored in a retrieval system, or transmitted, in any form or by any means,
without the prior permission in writing of Oxford University Press

Permission to perform this work in public (except in the course of divine worship)
should normally be obtained from a local performing right licensing organization,
unless the owner or the occupier of the premises being used already holds
a licence from such an organization. Likewise, permission to make and
exploit a recording of these works should be obtained from a
local mechanical copyright licensing organization

Enquiries concerning reproduction outside the scope of the above
should be directed to the Music Rights Department, Oxford University Press,
at music.permissions.uk@oup.com or at the address above

ISBN 978-0-19-357695-7

Music and text origination by Katie Johnston
Printed in Great Britain on acid-free paper by Halstan & Co. Ltd, Amersham, Bucks.

Composer's note

Sŭnāō is a set of three pieces designed to introduce young choirs to the Hindi/Urdu language. The word 'sŭnāō' translates as 'have me listen', but is closer in meaning to 'tell me' or 'sing for me'. The first song, 'Āō', invites us to share our musical traditions with one another, exploring changing open vowels and featuring a two-part canon in its central section. 'Khaṭṭar paṭṭar' uses a distinctive style of onomatopoeia to describe how we sometimes let our thoughts run out of control. Opening with a whispered section, it has a high rhythmic energy and continual sense of drive. By contrast, the gently flowing 'Behtā jā' encourages us not to be too hard on ourselves, contrasting dark and light within a soft dynamic palette. Each piece is designed to teach linguistic concepts of Hindi and musical concepts of Hindustani music, while reminding us to approach new ideas from a place of curiosity rather than of judgement.

This note may be reproduced as required for programme notes.

Duration: *c*.11 minutes

Sŭnāō is also available in versions for SATB and piano (ISBN 978–0–19–357696–4) and SSAA and piano (ISBN 978–0–19–357698–8).

Pronunciation Guide

A video pronunciation guide is available on a companion website: www.oup.com/sunaao

Vowels

ā as in car	i as in sit	ŭ as in good
a as in about	ī as in tree	u as in thumb
e as in fed	ĩ as in tree, with nasalization	ū as in food
ẽ as in fed, with nasalization	ō as in note	

Consonants (when different from English pronunciation)
t as in the (dental)
d as in the Spanish word dos or dónde (dental)
r as in the Spanish word rojo or rosa (flipped)

Sounds with no equivalents in Romance languages

Aspirated
To make the sounds "bh", "chh", "dh", "kh", and "th":
• begin to say the sound before the final h, so "b", "ch", "d" (dental as "dos"), "k", and "t" (dental as "the")
• as you make the sound, push extra air through it (if you hold your palm a few inches in front of your mouth, you should be able to feel a puff of air)

Retroflex
To make the sounds "ḍ" and "ṭ":
• curl your tongue back, so the underside of the tip is touching the top of your mouth (retroflex consonant)
• then bring it forward to pronounce the "ḍ" and "ṭ"
To make the sound "ṛ":
• curl your tongue back as above
• then flip your tongue forward as if saying both "r" and "d"

Texts and translations

These texts may be reproduced as required for programme notes.

1. Āō (आओ)

Āō	आओ
Ā-jāō	आ जाओ
Ā-ke dhŭn sŭnāō	आके धुन सुनाओ
Apnī āvāz le-āō	अपनी आवाज़ ले आओ
Alag andāz dikhāō	अलग अंदाज़ दिखाओ

Come
Come on
Come and sing us a tune

Bring your own voice
And show us a different style

2. Khaṭṭar paṭṭar (खट्टर पट्टर)

Bāhar se chīzē āyī—khaṭṭar paṭṭar	बाहर से चीज़ें आयीं—खट्टर पट्टर
Zamāne se bātē āyī—chakkar chakkar	ज़माने से बातें आयीं—चक्कर चक्कर
Khaṭṭar paṭṭar kō pīchhe chhōṛ	खट्टर पट्टर को पीछे छोड़
Dekh chakkar chakkar bhī rŭk gayā shōr	देख चक्कर चक्कर भी रुक गया शोर

Things come in from the outside—cling, clang
Chatter comes in from the world/times—spinning, spinning
Leave that cling-clanging behind you
See? The spinning has stopped, and so has the noise

3. Behtā jā (बहता जा)

Nā ḍāl khŭd pe tū zyādā zōr	ना डाल खुद पे तू ज़्यादा ज़ोर
Bhūl jāō dŭniyā kā shōr, ye sārā shōr	भूल जाओ दुनिया का शोर, ये सारा शोर
Nadī ke sāth behtā jā	नदी के साथ बहता जा
Havā ke sāth ŭṛtā jā	हवा के साथ उड़ता जा

Don't be too hard on yourself
Forget the noise of the world
Go on flowing with the river
Go on flying with the wind

Original Hindi texts by Reena Bhansali. Transliterations and English translations by Reena Bhansali and Reena Esmail.

Commissioned by a consortium through the Southern California Vocal Association

Sŭnāō
(सुनाओ)

Reena Bhansali (b. 1988)

REENA ESMAIL

1. Āō (आओ)
(Come)

* Grace notes with lines through should be placed before the beat. Those without lines through and with tenuto marks should be placed on the beat.
† Fanned beams indicate a gradual speeding up through the beamed group.
‡ Small notes indicate optional *divisi*.

© Oxford University Press 2025

Printed in Great Britain

OXFORD UNIVERSITY PRESS, MUSIC DEPARTMENT, GREAT CLARENDON STREET, OXFORD OX2 6DP
The Moral Rights of the Composer have been asserted. Photocopying this copyright material is ILLEGAL.

6
Ā - jā - ō ā - - - - jā - ō
Ā - jā - ō ā - - - - jā - ō
Ā - jā - ō ā - jā - ō ā - - jā - ō
8va
mp
p mp
p
accel.
rit. a tempo
11
p mf p mp
Ā - ke dhŭ - n dhŭ - - - n sŭ - nā - ō sŭ - nā - ō
p mf mp
Ā - ke dhŭ - n dhŭ - n sŭ - nā - ō
p mf p
Ā - ke dhŭ - n dhŭ - n sŭ - nā - ō
accel.
rit. a tempo
mf
p

* Small notes indicate optional *divisi*.

* Small notes indicate optional *divisi*.

* The second grace note should be played slightly after the left-hand chord has been struck, the top left-hand note also functioning as the first grace note, on the beat.

59
accel.
rit. a tempo
Ā - ke dhŭ - n dhŭ - - - n sŭ - nā - ō sŭ - nā - ō
Ā - ke dhŭ - n dhŭ - n sŭ - nā - ō sŭ-
Ā - ke dhŭ - n dhŭ - n sŭ - nā - ō sŭ-
accel.
rit. a tempo
65
sŭ - nā - ō sŭ - nā - ō
- nā - ō sŭ - nā - ō
- nā - ō sŭ - nā - ō
8va

2. Khaṭṭar paṭṭar (खट्टर पट्टर)
(Cling-clang)

* This movement should feel like it is just coming apart at the seams. The speed at which this will be felt will vary between choirs and performances, so conductors should pick a tempo accordingly.

† close to *m* immediately

© Oxford University Press 2025. Photocopying this copyright material is ILLEGAL.

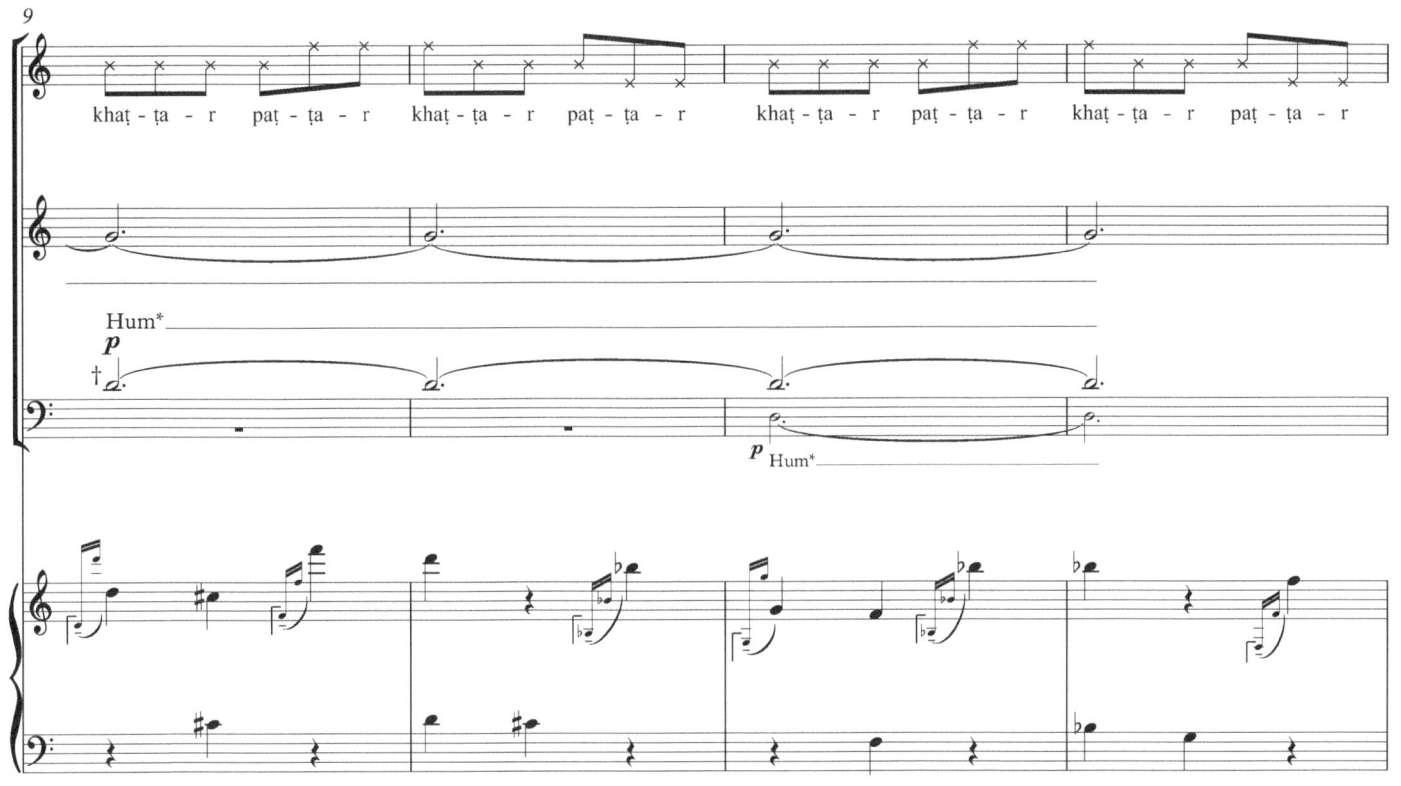

* close to *m* immediately

† Small notes/rests indicate optional *divisi*.

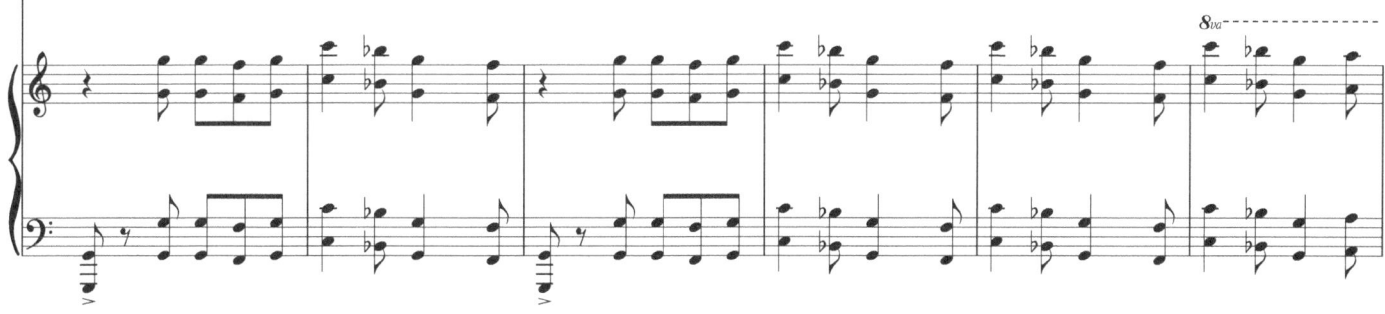

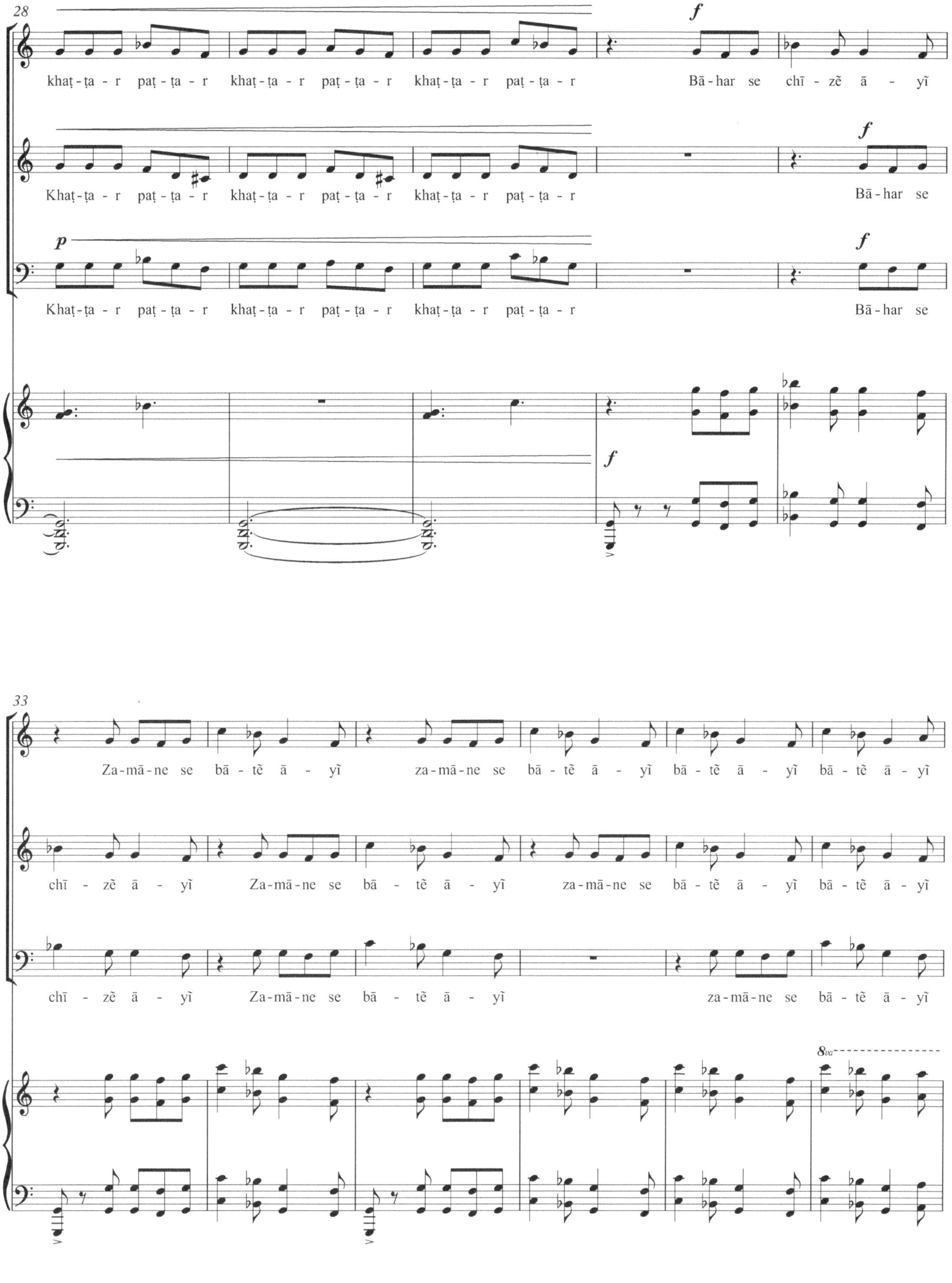
28
f
khaṭ - ṭa - r paṭ - ṭa - r khaṭ - ṭa - r paṭ - ṭa - r khaṭ - ṭa - r paṭ - ṭa - r Bā - har se chī - zẽ ā - yĩ
f
Khaṭ - ṭa - r paṭ - ṭa - r khaṭ - ṭa - r paṭ - ṭa - r khaṭ - ṭa - r paṭ - ṭa - r Bā - har se
p
f
Khaṭ - ṭa - r paṭ - ṭa - r khaṭ - ṭa - r paṭ - ṭa - r khaṭ - ṭa - r paṭ - ṭa - r Bā - har se
f
33
Za - mā - ne se bā - tẽ ā - yĩ za - mā - ne se bā - tẽ ā - yĩ bā - tẽ ā - yĩ bā - tẽ ā - yĩ
chī - zẽ ā - yĩ Za - mā - ne se bā - tẽ ā - yĩ za - mā - ne se bā - tẽ ā - yĩ bā - tẽ ā - yĩ
chī - zẽ ā - yĩ Za - mā - ne se bā - tẽ ā - yĩ za - mā - ne se bā - tẽ ā - yĩ
8va

* close to *m* immediately

* Small notes indicate optional *divisi*.

59
mp
Bā - har se chī - zē āyī Za - mā - ne se bā - tē bā - tē ā - yī Khaṭ - ṭa - r paṭ - ṭa - r
mp
Bā - har se chī - zē āyī Za - mā - ne se bā - tē bā - tē ā - yī Khaṭ - ṭa - r paṭ - ṭa - r
mp
Bā - har se chī - zē āyī Za - mā - ne se bā - tē bā - tē ā - yī Khaṭ - ṭa - r paṭ - ṭa - r
p
64
mf
f
khaṭ - ṭa - r paṭ - ṭa - r kō pī - chhe chhōṛ
f
khaṭ - ṭa - r paṭ - ṭa - r khaṭ - ṭa - r paṭ - ṭa - r khaṭ - ṭa - r paṭ - ṭa - r khaṭ - ṭa - r paṭ - ṭa - r khaṭ - ṭa - r paṭ - ṭa - r
f
khaṭ - ṭa - r paṭ - ṭa - r khaṭ - ṭa - r paṭ - ṭa - r khaṭ - ṭa - r paṭ - ṭa - r khaṭ - ṭa - r paṭ - ṭa - r khaṭ - ṭa - r paṭ - ṭa - r
f

79
mp
f
shōr khaṭ-ṭa-r paṭ-ṭa-r khaṭ-ṭa-r paṭ-ṭa-r khaṭ-ṭa-r paṭ-ṭa-r
shōr paṭ-ṭa-r khaṭ-ṭa-r paṭ-ṭa-r khaṭ-ṭa-r paṭ-ṭa-r khaṭ-ṭa-r paṭ-ṭa-r
p
shōr khaṭ-ṭa-r paṭ-ṭa-r khaṭ-ṭa-r paṭ-ṭa-r khaṭ-ṭa-r paṭ-ṭa-r chak-ka-r chak-ka-r

84
p
mp
chak-ka-r chak-ka-r chak-ka-r chak-ka-r Chum
chak-ka-r chak-ka-r Chum
mf
Khaṭ-ṭa-r paṭ-ṭa-r khaṭ-ṭa-r paṭ-ṭa-r
Chum
Khaṭ-ṭa-r paṭ-ṭa-r khaṭ-ṭa-r paṭ-ṭa-r
8va
mf dim.

3. *Behtā jā* (बहता जा)

(Flow)

* Grace notes with lines through should be placed before the beat. Those without lines through and with tenuto marks should be placed on the beat.
† Small notes indicate optional *divisi*.

© Oxford University Press 2025. Photocopying this copyright material is ILLEGAL.

10
Weighted
mp
Nā ḍā - l khŭ - d pe tū zyā - dā zōr
mp
Nā ḍā - l khŭ - d pe tū zyā - dā zōr
Weighted
p
14
mp
dŭ - ni - yā kā shōr ye sā - rā
Bhū - l jāō dŭ - ni - yā kā shōr
Bhū - l jāō dŭ - ni - yā kā shōr

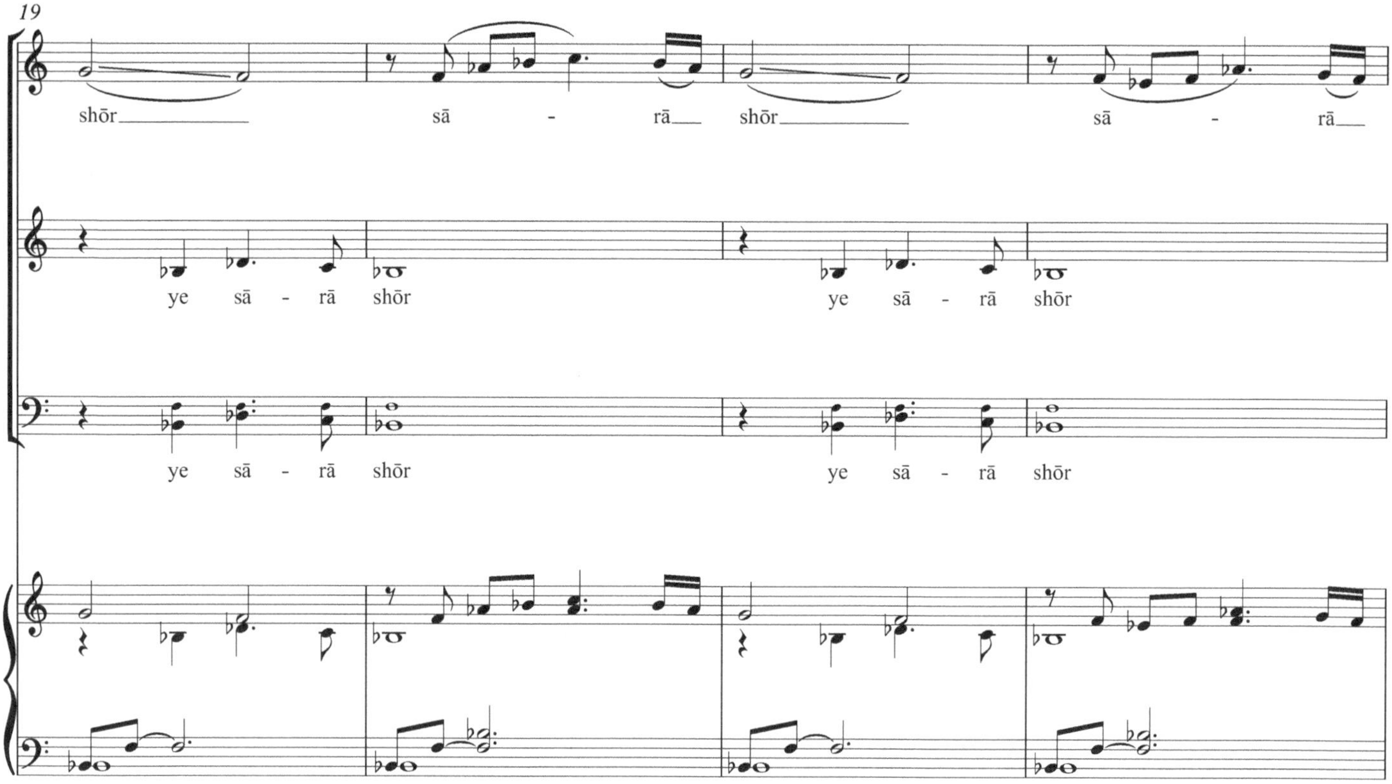
19
shōr sā - rā shōr sā - rā
ye sā - rā shōr ye sā - rā shōr
ye sā - rā shōr ye sā - rā shōr

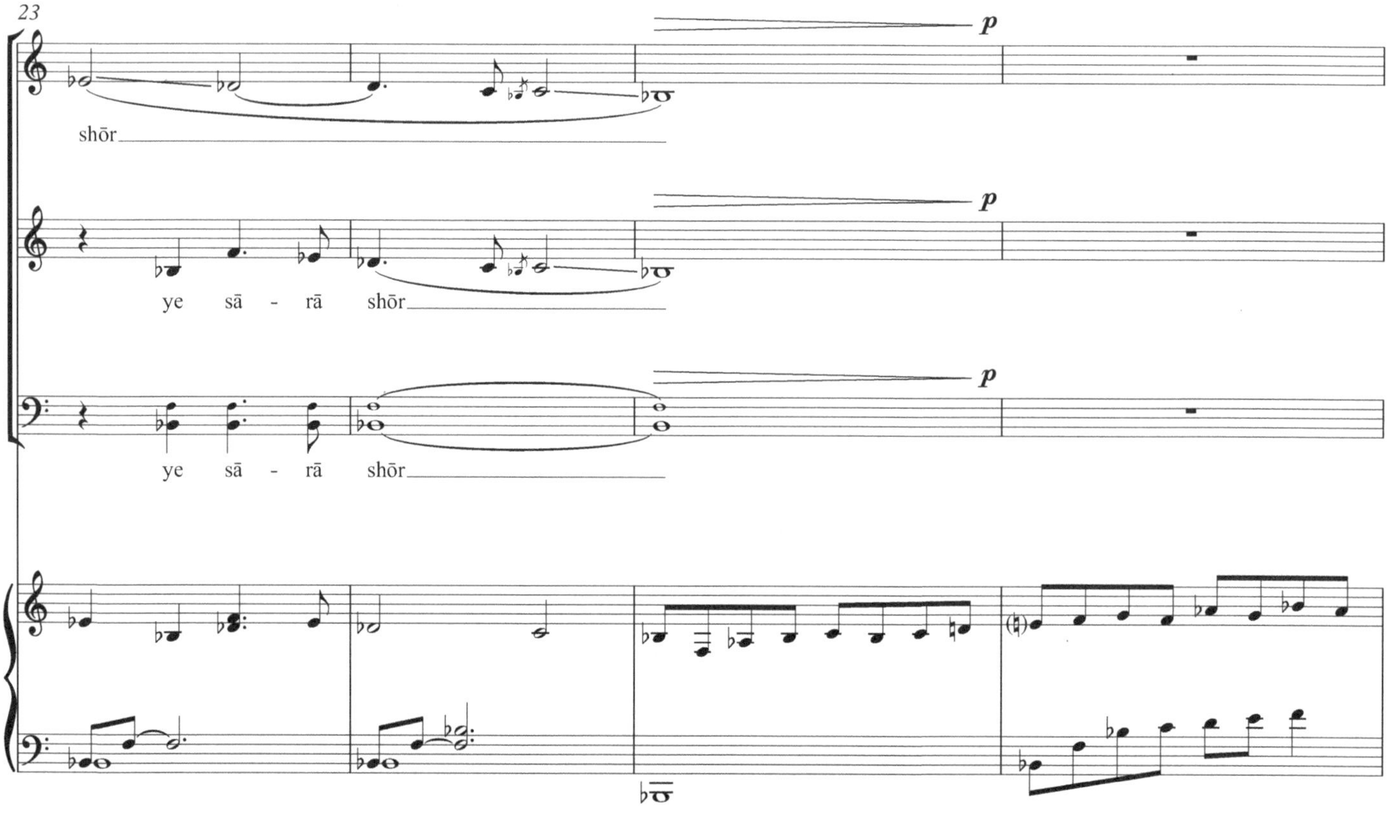
23
p
shōr
p
ye sā - rā shōr
p
ye sā - rā shōr

* An open 'e' vowel needs to be pronounced after the 'h' in the word 'behtā'.

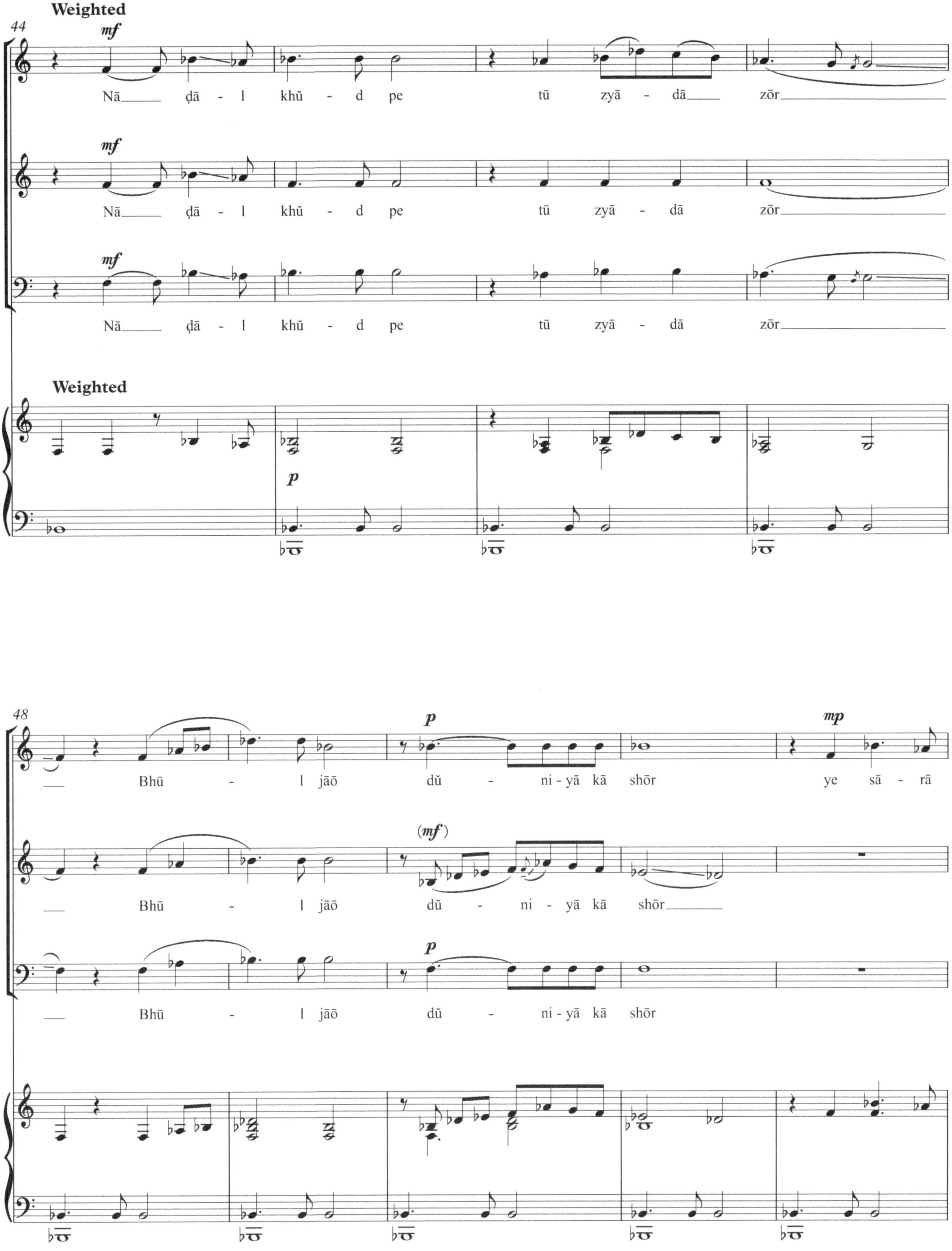
Weighted
44
mf
Nā ḍā - l khŭ - d pe tū zyā - dā zōr
mf
Nā ḍā - l khŭ - d pe tū zyā - dā zōr
mf
Nā ḍā - l khŭ - d pe tū zyā - dā zōr
Weighted
p
48
Bhū - l jāō dŭ - ni - yā kā shōr
p
mp
ye sā - rā
(mf)
Bhū - l jāō dŭ - ni - yā kā shōr
Bhū - l jāō dŭ - ni - yā kā shōr

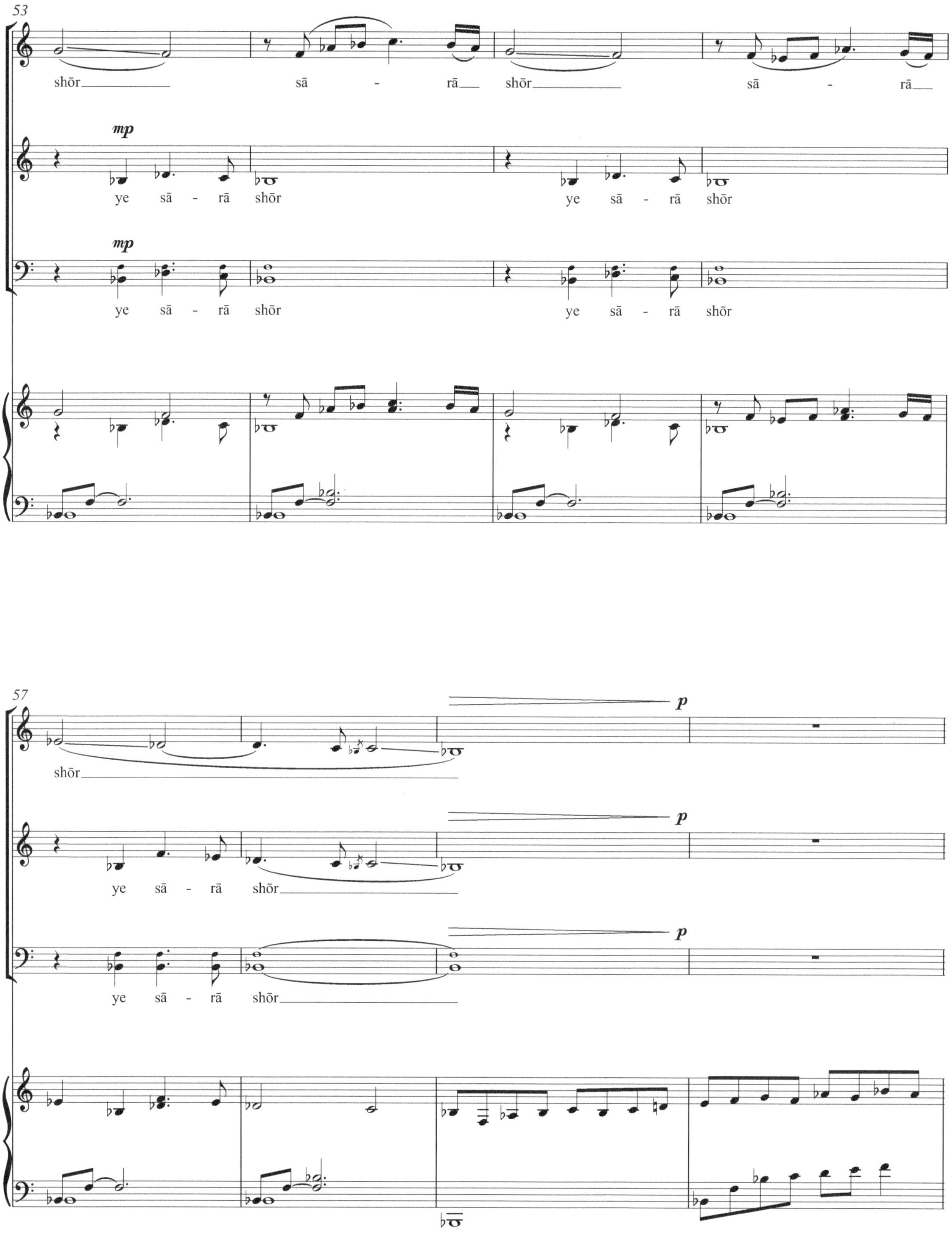

shōr_____ sā - rā__ shōr_____ sā - rā__

ye sā - rā shōr ye sā - rā shōr

ye sā - rā shōr ye sā - rā shōr

shōr_____

ye sā - rā shōr_____

ye sā - rā shōr_____

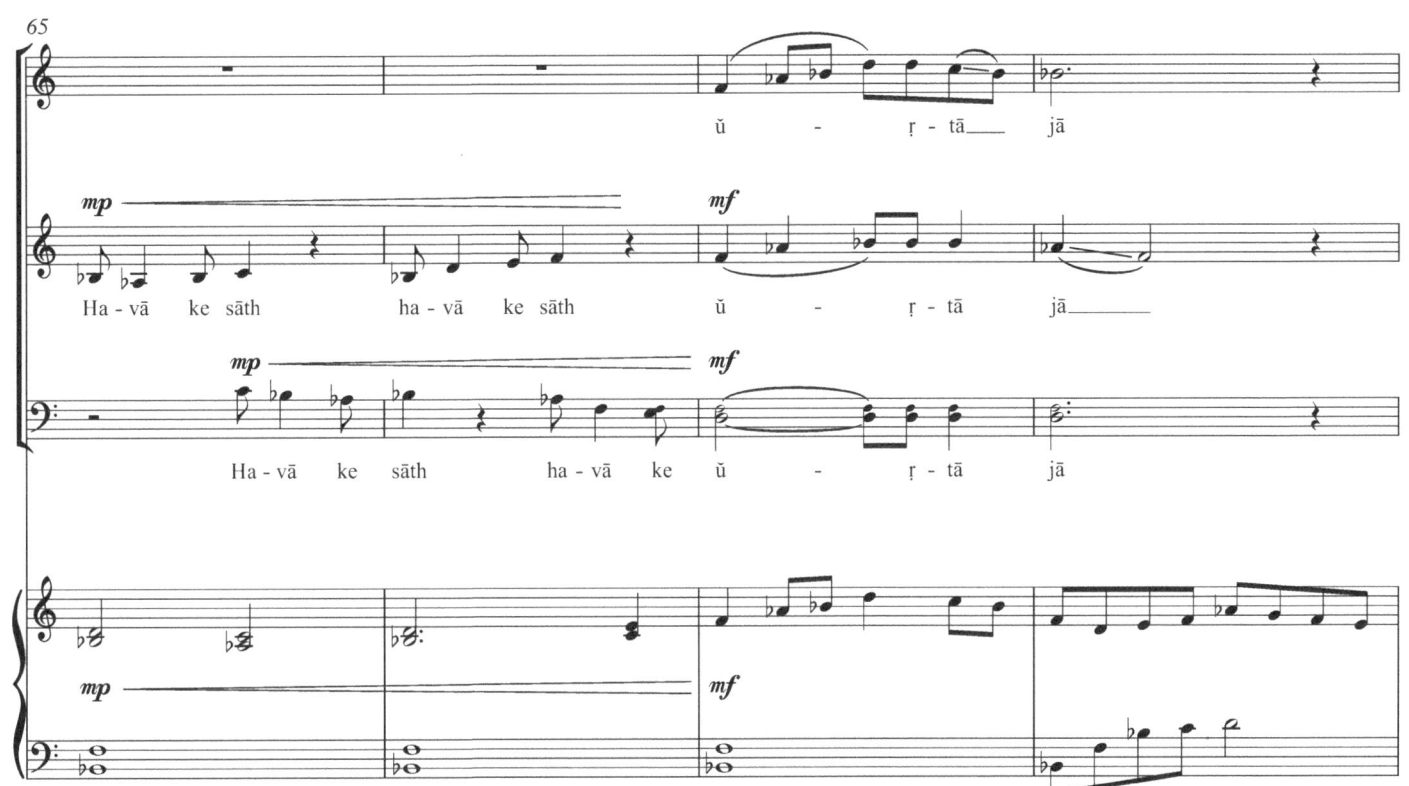

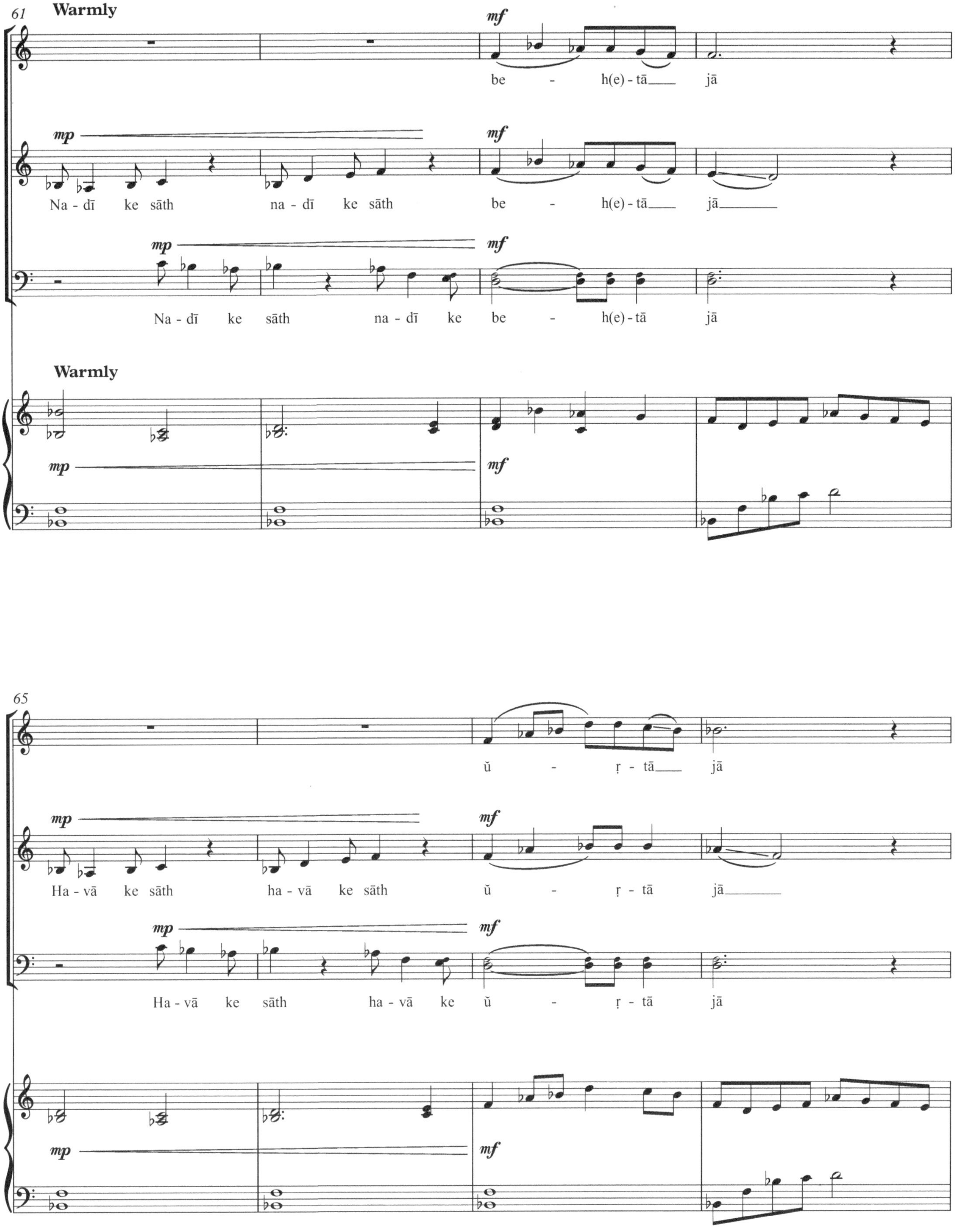
61
Warmly
mf
be - h(e) - tā jā
mp
mf
Na - dī ke sāth na - dī ke sāth be - h(e) - tā jā
mp
mf
Na - dī ke sāth na - dī ke be - h(e) - tā jā
Warmly
mp
mf
65
ŭ - ṛ - tā jā
mp
mf
Ha - vā ke sāth ha - vā ke sāth ŭ - ṛ - tā jā
mp
mf
Ha - vā ke sāth ha - vā ke ŭ - ṛ - tā jā
mp
mf

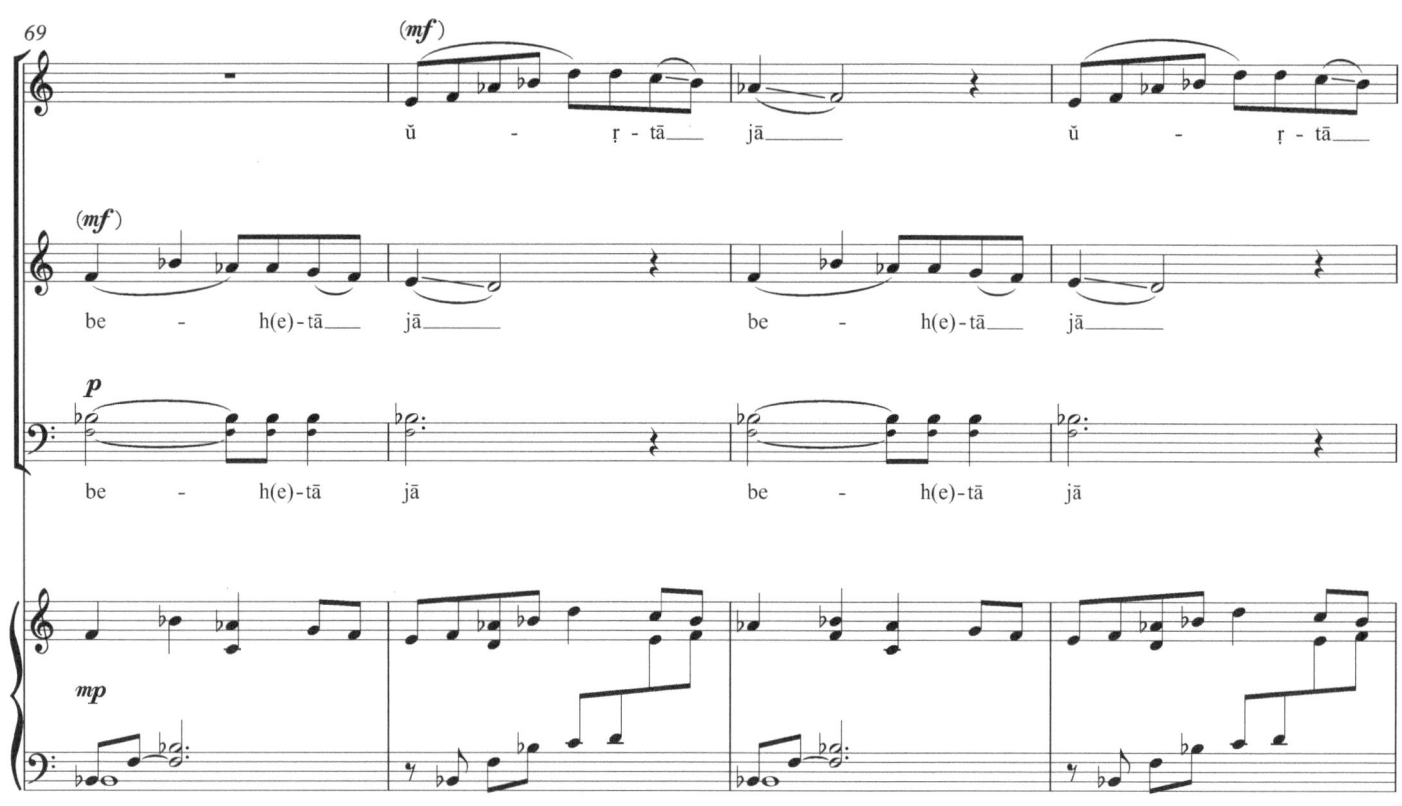

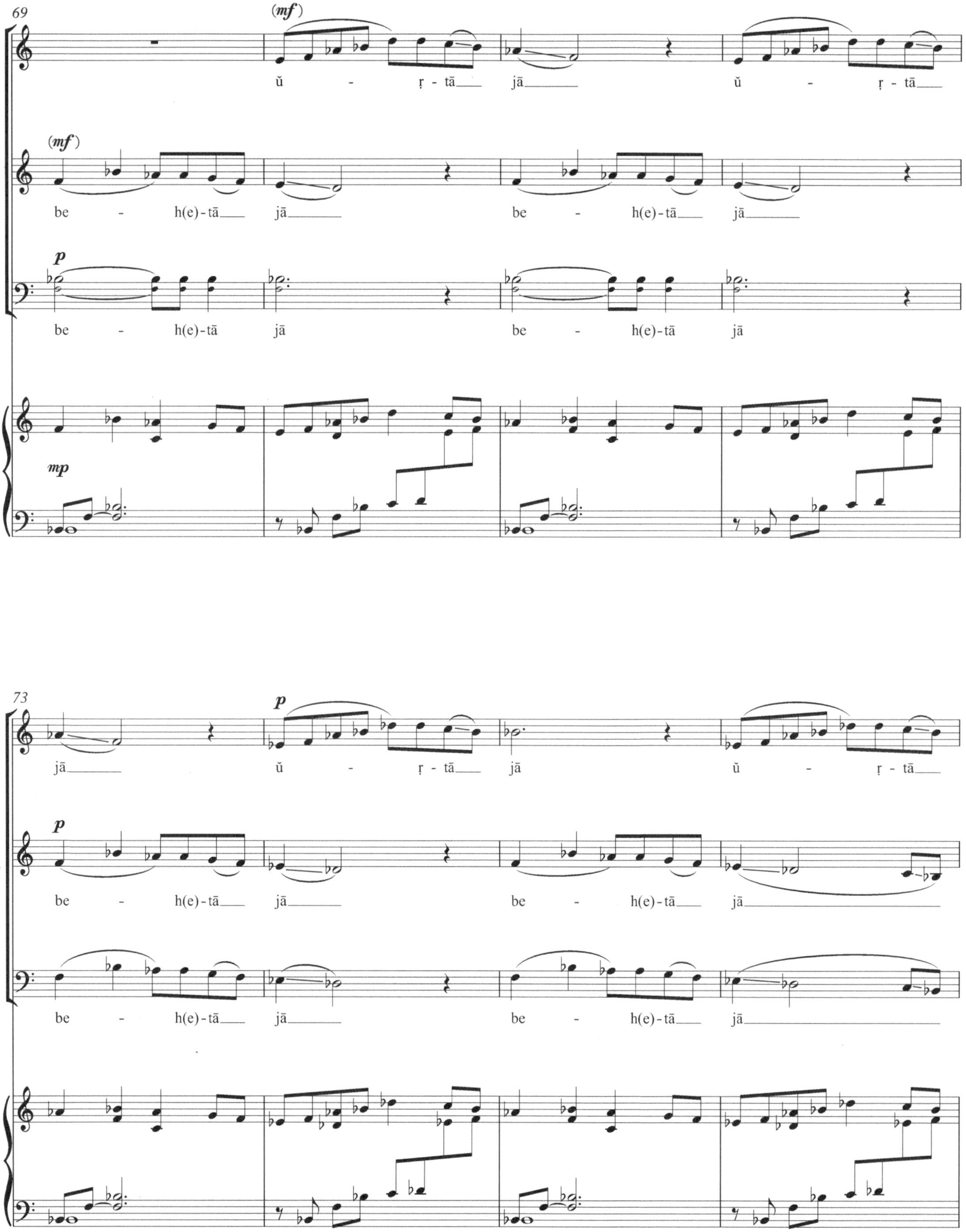
69
(mf)
ŭ - ṛ - tā jā ŭ - ṛ - tā
(mf)
be - h(e) - tā jā be - h(e) - tā jā
p
be - h(e) - tā jā be - h(e) - tā jā
mp
73
p
jā ŭ - ṛ - tā jā ŭ - ṛ - tā
p
be - h(e) - tā jā be - h(e) - tā jā
be - h(e) - tā jā be - h(e) - tā jā

* The soprano solo line may be sung by one soloist or a few voices; alternatively, it may be played on the piano (small notes).